PUFFIN BOOKS is part of the Penguin Random House group of companies
whose addresses can be found at global.penguinrandomhouse.com.

First published 2017
Copyright © Victoria and Albert Museum, London
Written by Anna Mason. The moral right of the author has been asserted
Printed in China   001
ISBN: 978–0–141–38722–2

Picture credits

Endpapers
Acanthus, William Morris, Jeffrey & Co.,
Morris & Co., London, UK, 1875.
V&A: E.496-1919
Given by Morris & Co.
Strawberry Thief, William Morris, Morris & Co.,
London, UK, 1883.
V&A: T.586-1919
Given by Morris & Co.

Imprint and title pages
Acanthus, William Morris, Jeffrey & Co.,
Morris & Co., London, UK, 1875.
V&A: E.496-1919
Given by Morris & Co.

Quote
Wild Tulip, William Morris, Jeffrey & Co.,
Morris & Co., England, UK, 1884.
V&A: E.538-1919
Given by Morris & Co.
Golden Legend, William Morris, Edward Coley
Burne-Jones, William Harcourt Hooper, Kelmscott
Press, Bernard Quaritch, London, UK, 1892.
V&A: E.1783-1920

A design hero
Anemone, William Morris, Morris & Co.,
Jeffrey & Co., England, UK, late 19th century.
V&A: E.736-1915
Given by Mr Allan F. Vigars
Photo of William Morris, Frederick Hollyer,
unknown, UK, 1884.
V&A: 7715-1938

Ideology and beliefs
Photo of William Morris, Frederick Hollyer,
(unknown), UK, 1873.
V&A: 7714-1938
Willow, William Morris, Jeffrey & Co.,
Morris & Co., England, UK, 1874.
V&A: E.493-1919
Given by Morris & Co.

Life story
Trellis, William Morris, Philip Speakman Webb,
Jeffrey & Co., Morris & Co., London, UK, 1862
(designed), 1864 (manufactured).
V&A: E.452-1919
Given by Morris & Co.

Morris the designer
Photo of the Morris room, V&A, London, UK, 1866.
Sussex chair, Philip Speakman Webb, Morris & Co.,
London, UK, ca. 1860 (designed), 1870-1890 (made).
V&A: CIRC.288-1960
Armchair, Ford Madox Brown, Morris & Co, London,
1870-1900
V&A: CIRC.28-1962
St George Cabinet, Philip Speakman Webb, William
Morris, Morris, Marshall, Faulkner & Co., London,
UK, 1861-1862.
V&A: 341:1 to 8-1906
Acanthus wall hanging, William Morris, Morris & Co.,
(unknown), UK, ca.1880.
V&A: T.153-1979

Morris the craftsman
Loom, Merton Abbey Workshop, England, UK, late
19th century.
V&A: 293-1893
Given by William Morris
Strawberry Thief (printing blocks), William Morris,
England, UK, 1883.
V&A: T.125B to W-1980
Photo of Morris & Co. Merton Abbey workshop
© William Morris Gallery

Inspired by nature
Autumn Leaves, William Morris, Morris & Co.,
Jeffrey & Co., England, UK, 1888.
V&A: E.567-1919
Given by Morris & Co.
Strawberry Thief, William Morris, Morris & Co.,
London, UK, 1883.
V&A: T.586-1919
Given by Morris & Co.
Daisy, William Morris, Morris & Co., Jeffrey & Co.,
England, UK, 1864.
V&A: E.2222-1913
Given by Sydney Vacher
Pimpernel, William Morris, Morris & Co.,
Jeffrey & Co., England, UK, 1876.
V&A: E.498-1919
Given by Morris & Co.

Exploring Morris's patterns
Strawberry Thief, William Morris,
Morris & Co., London, UK, 1883.
V&A: T.586-1919
Given by Morris & Co.
Little Chintz, William Morris, Morris & Co.,
London, UK, 1875.
V&A: T.40-1919
Wey, William Morris, Merton Abbey, UK,
ca.1883.
V&A: T.49-1912
Trellis, William Morris, Philip Speakman
Webb, London, UK, 1862.
V&A: E.452-1919

Wandle – pattern in focus
Wandle, William Morris, London, UK, 1884.
V&A: T.425-1934

Beyond Morris & Co.
Photograph of Hammersmith Socialist League
William Morris, England, UK, ca. 1888.
V&A: 1817-1938
'Proof page for The Kelmscott Chaucer',
Edward Coley Burne-Jones, William Morris,
William Harcourt Hooper, London, 1896.
V&A: E.1255-1912

The Arts and Crafts movement
St James's, William Morris, Jeffrey & Co.,
Morris & Co., England, UK, 1881.
V&A: E.528-1919
Given by Morris & Co.
Design for a poster, Walter Crane, UK, 1899.
V&A: E.4199-1915
Season ticket, Walter Crane, UK, 1890.
V&A: E.4164-1915
Given by Emslie John Horniman

The legacy
Wey, William Morris, Merton Abbey, UK,
ca.1883.
V&A: T.49-1912

Supporting the world's leading
museum of art and design,
the Victoria and Albert
Museum, London

WILLIAM MORRIS

ARTIST • DESIGNER • POET • CAMPAIGNER

Discover the world of art and design through the V&A Introduces series. The Victoria and Albert Museum is the world's leading museum of art and design and houses over 2.3 million objects spanning over 5,000 years of human creativity. Inspired by its exhibitions, collections and heroes, this collectible series brings the wonder of the designed world to all!

'History has remembered the kings and warriors, because they destroyed; art has remembered the people, because they created.'

William Morris

A design hero

Artist, designer, poet, campaigner: William Morris was all of these things. Born in 1834, Morris believed in 'art for all' and that beauty had the power to change everyday lives.

With his interior design company Morris & Co., he called for a return to crafts, the use of natural – rather than man-made – materials, and designs that were both practical and beautiful. Morris's love of pattern, colour and texture was always evident in the textiles, wallpapers and furniture he created. He also found time to campaign for a better society and write poetry – in fact, he was more famous for his writings than his designs when he was alive!

William Morris's functional design, use of natural materials and high standards of craftsmanship continue to inspire artists today, while his designs – both original and reimagined – still captivate the imagination of contemporary society.

Ideology and beliefs

**'I do not want art for a few, any more than
education for a few, or freedom for a few'**

Morris believed that art was an essential part of a
meaningful life. He argued that all children should be
taught to draw, as well as read and write.

**'To apply art to useful wares . . .
is not a frivolity, but part of the serious
business of life'**

One of Morris's greatest legacies was his belief that design
should be taken seriously and required as much artistic skill
as traditional fine arts, like painting and sculpture.

**'Have nothing in your houses that you do not
know to be useful, or believe to be beautiful'**

Morris felt that mass production encouraged people to be
wasteful. He thought we should have fewer possessions and
that they should have a purpose, bring us pleasure and be
designed to last.

'It is the allowing of machines to be our masters and not our servants that so injures the beauty of life nowadays'

Morris believed that technology was removing valuable skills rather than saving time and labour.

'The past is not dead, it is living in us, and will be alive in the future which we are now helping to make'

Morris always had one eye on the past and one on the future. He studied ancient textiles and designs – not to copy them, but to inspire new creativity.

'No man is good enough to be another's master'

Morris believed in social equality and the right for all men and women to lead independent lives. In the 1880s he became one of the leaders of the early socialist movement and an active campaigner.

'Fellowship is life, and lack of fellowship is death'

Though a fiery character, Morris was warm and loyal to his friends. He liked to work with others, believing different creative skills gave the best results.

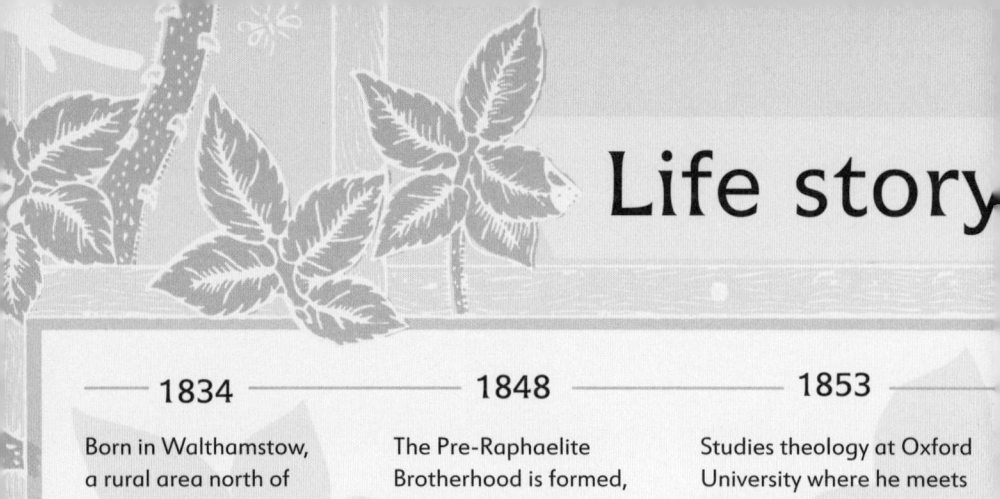

Life story

1834

Born in Walthamstow, a rural area north of London. Develops a love of nature as a child exploring Epping Forest.

1848

The Pre-Raphaelite Brotherhood is formed, pioneering a radical new approach to art.

1853

Studies theology at Oxford University where he meets Edward Burne-Jones. Soon after, the two friends decide to dedicate their lives to art.

1868

Publishes his most famous work of poetry, *The Earthly Paradise*, and becomes a household name.

1875

Morris takes sole control of the business, renamed Morris & Co. The fashionable department store Liberty & Co. opens on Regent Street.

1877

Founds the Society for the Protection of Ancient Buildings. Morris & Co. opens a showroom on Oxford Street.

1859

Marries Jane Burden, skilled embroiderer, Pre-Raphaelite muse and daughter of an Oxford stableman.

1860

Moves to Red House in Bexleyheath, a red brick medieval-style home built for the Morris family by their close friend Philip Webb.

1861

Decides to start a decorating business called Morris, Marshall, Faulkner & Co., with a group of friends. His first daughter, Jenny, is born; May follows a year later.

1883

Shocks many of his friends by becoming a revolutionary socialist; starts campaigning for social equality.

1891

Founds the Kelmscott Press to produce beautiful books.

1896

Dies in London aged 62. His doctor claims 'the disease is simply being William Morris and having done more work than most ten men'.

Other exciting things going on at the time:

1838 Coronation of Queen Victoria
1848 London Waterloo station opens
1861 *Great Expectations* is written by Charles Dickens
1859 National Portrait Gallery opens
1867 Karl Marx writes *Capital: A Critique of Political Economy*
1874 Major Impressionist art exhibition in Paris with works by Monet, Degas and Renoir
1879 Thomas Edison invents the light bulb

Morris the designer

William Morris started his design career by creating objects for his own home. His company, Morris & Co., offered customers wallpapers, stained glass, furniture, hand-painted tiles, embroideries, carpets and tapestries. Clients could choose from ready-made items or ask for one-off designs.

Furniture

Morris thought that everyday furniture should be simple and well made. The company's popular range of Sussex chairs were light and elegant, with woven rush seats and slender dark-wood frames. For the most important rooms in the house, Morris & Co. also offered more elaborate, medieval-style furniture, hand-painted or decorated with leather and gold.

St George cabinet

Sussex chairs

Wallpapers

Morris started designing wallpapers in the 1860s that were block-printed by hand, giving a richly textured surface. Morris's company produced a wide range of wallpaper designs, many of which are still popular today.

Stained glass

Stained glass for decorating churches and houses was an important part of the business. Morris admired the techniques used to produce medieval stained glass and wanted his windows to be just as impressive. He used jewel-like colours and collaborated on the designs with other artists, especially Edward Burne-Jones.

Textiles

Morris's love of pattern, colour and texture came together in his work with cloth. He revived ancient methods of dyeing, printing and weaving, as well as experimented with new techniques. Morris & Co. offered embroidered hangings and cushion covers, printed fabric for curtains and upholstery, woven hangings in wool and silk, and richly textured hand-knotted rugs.

Wall hanging

Morris the craftsman

Natural dyes

Victorian textile manufacturers used chemical dyes to produce bright colours cheaply. Morris thought these colours were unnaturally bright, and he disliked the way they also faded quickly. To achieve the rich, deep tones he wanted, he used natural plant and vegetable dyes. Two of his favourite colours were madder red and indigo blue.

Tapestry

Morris thought of tapestry as the 'noblest of the weaving arts' because of the rich colour, variation of texture and subtle detail that could be achieved. Tapestries were woven by hand on upright looms using naturally dyed yarns. They would take months to weave and were only affordable for Morris's wealthier clients. Nevertheless, he succeeded in bringing this long-neglected art form back into fashion.

Weaving

At Merton Abbey, Morris used hand-operated looms to produce a huge variety of silk and wool woven fabrics. Weaving is more complicated than printing and Morris delighted in the different textures he was able to achieve. Some of his most successful designs, especially 'Peacock and Dragon', were extremely luxurious.

Carpet weaving loom

Woodblock printing

Morris & Co.'s wallpapers and printed cottons were block-printed by hand, which required skill and hard work. Each woodblock was prepared by carving away areas to leave a raised pattern, which would pick up the dye (like a stamp). The most complicated and colourful designs required over thirty different woodblocks to print. Each block had a metal pin on the corners to help line up the design accurately. Exactly the right amount of pressure had to be applied to transfer the pigment on to the paper or cloth. Once a length had been printed, it was left to dry before the next colour could be applied.

Woodblocks used to create the 'Strawberry Thief' pattern

Inspired by nature

Morris's patterns were inspired by nature and the countryside. Wild and garden flowers, birds and animals all feature in his designs. As a young child growing up in the Essex countryside, he was given his own plot of garden to look after and quickly learnt the names and shapes of different plants. He avoided exotic species in his designs, choosing the English flowers and plants he could observe first hand.

Morris's patterns use natural images to remind us of the outdoors but he never copied nature literally. Instead, plants and flowers are simplified, using clear outlines, symmetry and a limited colour palette.

Strawberry Thief

'Strawberry Thief' is one of Morris's most popular designs. The pattern was inspired by the birds in his garden that used to creep under the net and eat the strawberries before they could be picked.

Daisy

'Daisy' was the first William Morris wallpaper to be sold, in 1864. It is a design that includes meadow flowers.

Pimpernel

This design is called 'Pimpernel' after the plant. Morris used the small yellow flowers to create this detailed pattern.

Exploring Morris's patterns

A pattern occurs when shapes or other elements are repeated to make a design. Morris was a master of designing flat patterns. He was so good that it's often hard to spot where the repeat starts and ends.

Colour

In nature, every plant and flower is made up of thousands of subtle shades and tints of colour. However, in his wallpapers and textiles, Morris chose to use a restricted colour palette rather than copy nature exactly, often favouring the combination of red and blue found in Indian textiles.

Symmetry

Many things in nature are symmetrical, from the wings of a butterfly to snowflakes. Morris used symmetry in many of his patterns, including 'Strawberry Thief'.

Structure

If you look closely, you'll see that every pattern has a framework that holds all the elements together. Having a framework in a pattern doesn't necessarily make it look too rigid or controlled. In fact, many similar frameworks and patterns can be seen in nature or the garden. Here are a few of the frameworks most often used in Morris's patterns.

A diamond-net pattern is found in nature on the skin of snakes and other reptiles. Morris's 'Little Chintz' also has this pattern.

Branches and the veins of leaves often grow diagonally, a pattern replicated in Morris's 'Wey' pattern.

A trellis is a square grid that plants grow on. Morris was inspired to create 'Trellis' by the rose-trellis in the garden of his house in Bexleyheath.

Wandle – pattern in focus

William Morris named this pattern in honour of the river that ran near his workshops at Merton Abbey in Surrey. The Wandle provided the supply of fresh running water that he needed for dyeing and printing cloth.

Structure

The pattern is based on strong diagonal lines created by the wide striped stems that run through it . Smaller, more delicately intertwined stems soften the effect. Because of their size and colour, the large flower heads on the diagonal lines take prominence over the small blue-and-white flowers in the background layer. The repeat is the largest Morris ever attempted for a printed textile and required thirty-two blocks to print.

Line

As in all of his designs, Morris uses a clear outline here, so each stem, leaf and petal is clear to see. Small dots (created through pins tapped into the surface of the woodblock) add texture, and the blue lines on the petals suggest a sense of movement. Morris told people who wanted to be pattern designers: 'Do not involve yourself in a tangle of poor weak lines that people can't make out . . . '

Colour

This is one of Morris's most colourful printed textiles but he still used only a few colours to make the chrysanthemums stand out. The principal colours are indigo blue and shades of madder red, with small highlights in green and yellow.

Design

The 'Wandle' design was inspired by historic textiles, which often featured a strong diagonal branch with flowers springing from it. The large flower heads are stylized chrysanthemums.

Beyond Morris & Co.

As well as designing for Morris & Co., William Morris achieved many things during his life. The same values that influenced his designs also influenced his other work: his belief in 'art for all', his love of nature and dislike of factories, and his respect for the past.

A fairer society

In the 1880s, Morris joined the Democratic Federation to become one of the leaders of the early socialist movement. The Democratic Federation's manifesto called for better housing for workers, free education for children and an eight-hour working day. Morris travelled across the country to speak on the subject of equality and put his artistic skills to good use by designing the Democratic Federation membership card! Morris founded the Socialist League in 1884, but eventually parted ways with the organization because of their increasingly violent tactics.

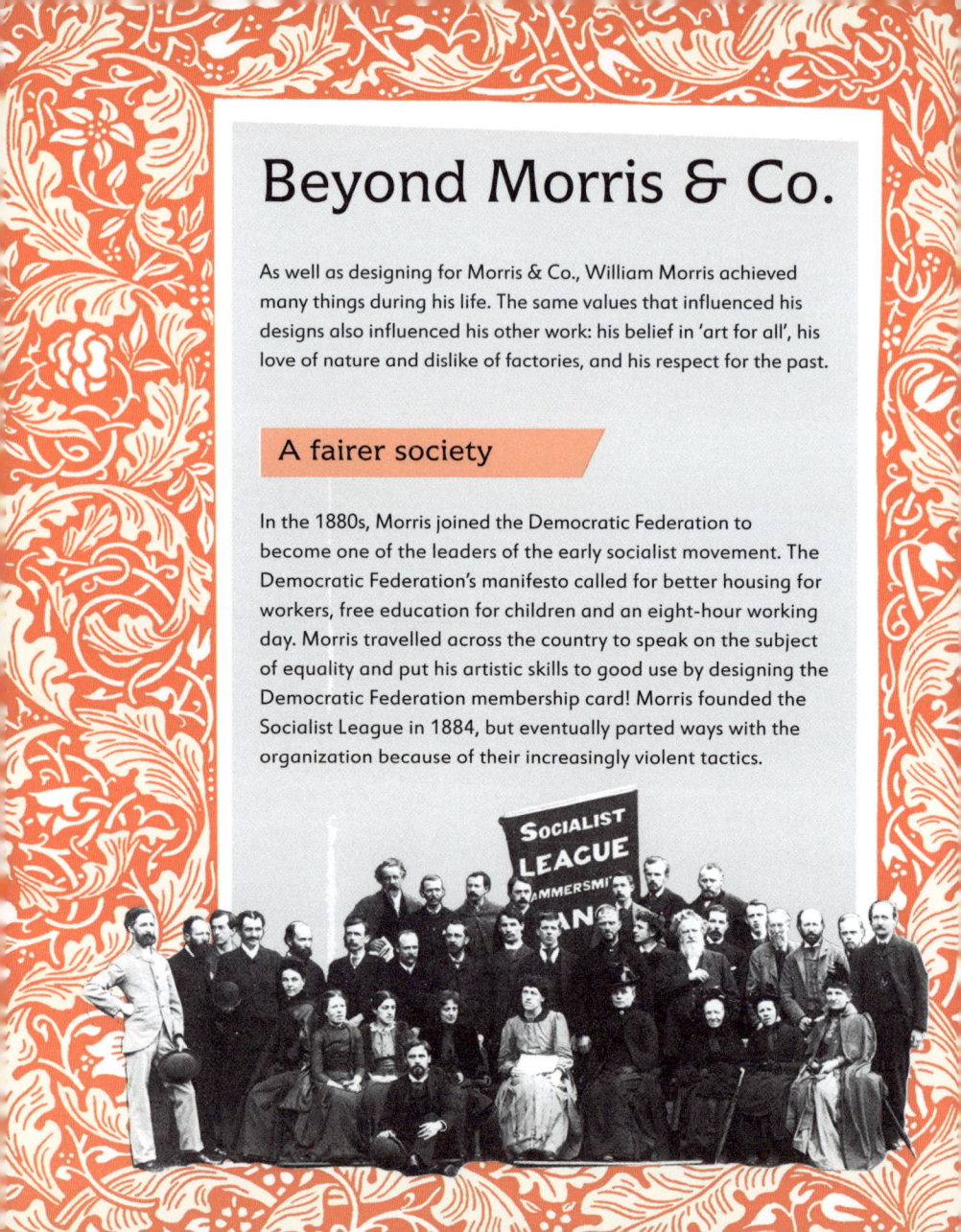

Membership card

Again, Morris was inspired by nature in his design, using acorns and oak trees to symbolize what people could achieve together.

Poetry

William Morris wrote all his life. His first poetry collection, *The Defence of Guenevere and Other Poems*, was published in 1858, when Morris was just twenty-four years old. Through his work, he showed his love of the past, writing long poems based on stories from hundreds of years ago. *The Earthly Paradise*, one of Morris's best-known works, is about a group of Norsemen who set sail to seek a land 'where none grow old'. Morris sometimes created designs or illustrations for his books too.

Kelmscott Press

William Morris believed the standards of printed books were slipping so, in 1891, he founded the Kelmscott Press with the aim of producing books that had a 'definite claim to beauty'. Similar to how he revived traditional techniques when creating his designs, Morris looked at how the earliest books were printed and copied those methods, always using handmade paper and creating his own typeface. *The Kelmscott Chaucer* was illustrated by Edward Burne-Jones and took four years to make!

The Arts and Crafts movement

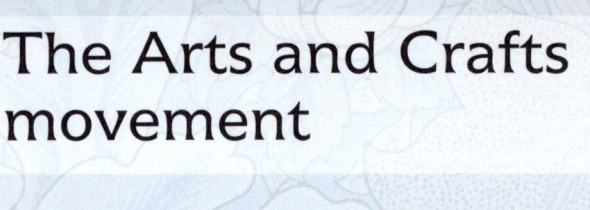

The Arts and Crafts movement began in Britain around 1880, inspired by the ideas of William Morris and the art critic John Ruskin. A younger generation of designers and architects believed art and craft could improve people's lives. The movement celebrated craft skills and the natural beauty of materials over cheaply produced goods, and turned the home into a work of art. These ideas quickly spread to Europe, America and Japan.

A better society

The movement also wanted to make society better. Small-scale craft industries sprung up, offering training and employment for local people. Horrified by working conditions in large factories, Arts and Crafts designers thought that work should be creative, fun and varied.

Love of nature

Like Morris, many Arts and Crafts designers turned to nature for inspiration. Some even left the city and set up their workshops in the countryside, hoping for a simpler way of life. Many designers were worried that industrialization was damaging the environment and tried to work in a way that wouldn't harm nature, for example by using local materials.

Ideals and aspirations

Arts and Crafts designers believed that everyday objects deserved as much thought and attention as painting and sculpture. They enjoyed traditional skills, including woodwork, ceramics, metalwork, book design, textiles and gardening. They thought that successful design required a thorough understanding of materials and techniques, and often made things themselves by hand. New art schools were founded to teach practical skills.

The legacy

Design

One of Morris's greatest legacies is his belief that homes should be beautiful. Over 150 years since he founded his company, his wallpaper and textile designs are still appearing in people's homes. While the original patterns remain popular, contemporary artists and printmakers have also played with Morris's designs to give them a more modern look. Many wallpaper designers have been inspired by Morris to create their own styles.

Garden cities

Morris believed that everyone should have the same access to nature that he had as a child. In a lecture called 'Town and Country' in 1894, he proposed the idea of small, self-sufficient rural communities. This idea took hold and in 1903 the first garden city – Letchworth – was created. Surrounded by greenery, with space for people to grow their own food, the city offered a new type of healthy living.

'WHAT BUSINESS HAVE WE WITH ART AT ALL UNLESS ALL CAN SHARE IT?'

Arts and crafts

Morris found joy in being a practical hands-on craftsman. The Arts and Crafts movement continued after his death, in the work of designers such as C. R. Ashbee and architects like C. F. A. Voysey. Today, 'hand-made' and 'artisan' products are often considered to be better than goods made in a factory.

William Morris was a creative force who pioneered new ideas about the relationship between art and everyday life. Morris's legacy – his belief in the power of beauty and how it can transform lives – continues to influence the design world, and society, to this day.